Second Edition

F.L.I.P.P.

(Faithful Learning in Public and Private)

Your Life

Kimbralon Barnes

Illustrated By Chad Thompson

Halo
PUBLISHING
INTERNATIONAL

Halo Publishing International
7550 WIH-10 #800, PMB 2069,
San Antonio, TX 78229

Second Edition, July 2024
ISBN: 978-1-63765-664-8

Halo Publishing International is a self-publishing company that publishes adult fiction and non-fiction, children's literature, self-help, spiritual, and faith-based books. Do you have a book idea you would like us to consider publishing? Please visit www.halopublishing.com for more information.

Wow! It is hard to believe that it has been ten years since I wrote this book. *F.L.I.P.P. Your Life* has been an awesome book to read, alongside your Bible of course, for a long time. My dedication list has grown throughout my own journey with God.

To God, the driver of my car. Thank you for loving us and gifting us with your Son, our Lord and Savior Jesus Christ, and a purpose to fulfill on Earth. You have kept my car clean with Your love, grace, and mercy.

To my parents, Louis and Helen, who nurtured and encouraged me to be the greatest writer, counselor, mother, and whatever I want to be. A big *beep beep*—which means thank you. I love you both so much.

To my husband, John, aka Gus, for being the best passenger by my side. For supporting me, encouraging me, wiping my tears, and believing in me while I wrote this book.

To my sedans, aka children, Chelsea, Kayla, Kevin, Demetrius, Malcom, Madison, and Trevon. I pray for peace and joy in all of your journeys.

To my dearest friends, Carla, Tabitha, Sade, Elaine, and Choyce, for believing that I could write a book, praying for me, cheering for me, and going on countless trips to promote this book.

A special dedication to Bishop B. Derone Robinson, whose encouragement, inspiration, and guidance contributed to the birth of this book. To Pastor Bobby J. Loving for the amazing support and words of encouragement. Though none of you are physically present, your spirits live within this book.

This book is dedicated to my coupes, aka grandchildren, Eri'Yan, Jeremiah, Erijah, Sarai, Ayden, Stefon, Ylan, Kairo, Serena, Alexander, Riley and Demi. I pray that my little cars experience a wonderful journey with God.

To those who are reading this book. I pray it helps you on your journey with God.

TABLE OF CONTENTS

.

Preface for Adults

Greetings Parents, Guardians, Pastors, Church Workers, and other adults! **F.L.I.P.P. (Faithful Learning In Public and Private) Your Life** is a book designed to assist children ages 9 to 12 but it is appropriate for younger children with adult assistance. It is essential because pictorial associations are used to encourage children to elevate their relationship with God. The car parts assist with memorization concepts and make learning more enjoyable. Children will learn the meaning of salvation and essential components required to grow in their relationship with Jesus Christ. The association between the component and car part will allow the children to retain the information and encourage them to share God's Word with others fulfilling the Great Commission (Matthew 28:19-20).

Preface for Children

Hello, thanks for picking me to read. If you are looking for a cool book to read, you found it! I hope you will read me over and over again. What am I about? I am glad you asked! **F.L.I.P.P. (Faithful Learning In Public and Private) Your Life** is a book that will help you build a strong friendship with Jesus Christ by discussing parts of Christianity using parts of a car. Christianity? Car parts? How does that work? You will have to take me home to find out how it works and share this really cool book with others.

CHAPTER 1: HOW DO I FLIPP MY LIFE?

"Therefore, I urge you, brothers and sisters, in view of God's mercy, to offer your bodies as a living sacrifice, holy and pleasing to God—this is your true and proper worship. Do not conform to the pattern of this world, but be transformed by the renewing of your mind. Then you will be able to test and approve what God's will is—his good, pleasing and perfect will." Romans 12:1-2 NIV

Hello, Friend! Thank you for taking time out to read this book. Are you ready to **F.L.I.P.P.** your life? This book is exactly what you need to help you *flip* your life and become Christ-like as you get older on your journey as a Christian. What does it mean to be Christ-like? (Hint: Go get your Bible if you do not have it. There will be Scriptures throughout the book, but it will be fun to find the Scripture in your own Bible.) Your Bible may have different words, but the meaning of the Scripture is the same. The first Scripture is Romans 12:1-2. Paul, one of God's special leaders, or disciples, wrote a message from God for people who gave their lives to Jesus Christ. Paul wanted the people to know that living for God is being a good example to others such as showing respect to adults or your peers, following the rules, and reading your Bible.

It also means to make good choices and not do bad things that may hurt others like telling mean jokes or making fun of people, bullying, or lying. Christianity, being a follower of Jesus Christ, is like trading your old car for a new one or rebuilding an old car.

Old cars may have rust, dents or scratches on the outside or have mechanical problems that cost a lot of money to repair. Some car owners may want to change cars or fix up their old ones to drive something new and exciting. New cars, or old cars that have been repaired, are dependable, look and smell good, and will run for a long time with good maintenance.

Christianity trades in the bad things we have done in the past for a new life with Jesus Christ. Our new life gives us a chance to make good choices and be a good example for others. You are about to learn some important things as a Christian to become more Christ-like using different parts of a car. Buckle your seat belt and get ready for the ride of your life!

When you hear the word *flip*, you may think of someone flipping a burger, which turns the burger from one side to another. Also, people will *flip* their old car by painting and fixing it to look new. The *flip* in your life will help you turn in the right direction and start making good decisions.

The word **F.L.I.P.P.** in this book is an acronym. An acronym is a word that is made from the first letters of a group of words. In this book, **F.L.I.P.P.** stands for **F**aithful **L**earning **I**n **P**ublic and **P**rivate (see the FLIP in the group of words?) Faithful Learning In Public and Private sounds like a big "I don't understand…can I borrow a dictionary" sentence but it is not that bad…I promise.

Faithful Learning In Public and Private means being a God-like example to others while at church, or school and even while you are at home in your room. You have to remember that it does not matter where you are because God knows and sees everything. This book is the best book, second to the Bible, you will own because it is going to teach you how to be a God-like example and important things you need to do as a new Christian.

When you give your life to Jesus Christ, you do not wear a halo or grow wings because you said the prayer of faith. An important fact you have to remember is that you are not perfect. I know you are thinking,"What do you mean that I am not perfect? This book is supposed to help me and not put me down." There was one person that lived on the Earth who was perfect and His name is Jesus Christ. He sacrificed His perfect life by going to the cross to give us another chance to make good choices, live a Christ-like life, and be a positive example to others.

Although you are a Christian, you will still have good days, bad days, happy days, sad days, and angry days. You may still make bad choices or decisions, and people may do things that are bad or hurtful to you. You have to keep a Christ-like attitude in any situation because you are a Child of God.

Keep on reading this book because you will learn the things you need to do to keep your car (your life) running smoothly even when you hit bumps in the road.

Chapter 2: Can a Car really teach me about God?

"Lead me in your truth and teach me, for you are the God of my salvation; for you I wait all the day long."
Psalms 25:5 NIV

The answer is YES! A car can teach you about God and help you remember what you need to do as a new Christian. Engineers make cars with structures that are strong enough to hold all of its parts together while people drive them to different places. The structure of the car has to be strong enough to withstand all types of weather and road conditions to make sure people arrive to their destination safely.

Guess what? People operate like cars except one is human and the other is metal.

Huh?

I am glad you asked.

Our faith in God and the Bible make up the structure that keeps us together during good and bad times. Most people been inside of a car and know the different names of car parts. Using the different car parts will help you learn and remember things you need to do to be a Christ-like example to the world.

Cars have many parts that are responsible for performing

certain actions to keep passengers safe. However, there are some parts that more important because they have to be working properly at all times to protect passengers from harm and danger. Christians perform positive actions, such as being respectful and making good decisions to show the love of God to others. However, we have to do things for ourselves to help build our relationship with Jesus Christ. Even as a preteen, you are able to show people of all ages that God is so awesome and other people you meet will want to give their life to Christ, too.

If you received this book, you may have already given your life to Christ and are now ready to learn more about becoming a new Christian. This book uses a **car** to represent YOU and the steps you need to take to have a true friendship with God. Once you give your life to Jesus Christ, you are a Child of God and God loves his children. As you begin your journey as a new Christian, learn about the parts of YOUR car for a smooth ride.

Romans 10:9

2 Corinthians 5:7

John 8:12

Galatians 5:25

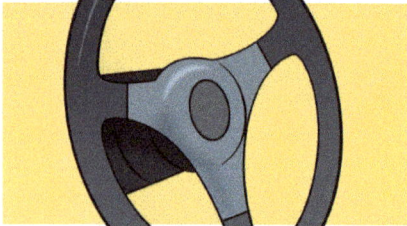

Philippians 4:6

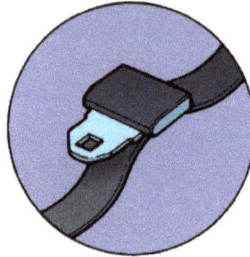

Proverbs 4:23

2 Timothy 3:16–17

Matthew 6:14

CHAPTER 3: THE KEY (SALVATION)

"If you declare with your mouth 'Jesus is Lord,' and believe in your heart that God raised him from the dead, you will be saved." Romans 10:9 NIV

In order to start your car, you have to have a key. The key represents giving your life to Christ to have eternal life in Heaven. This is a very important step. You must have the key in order to start your journey with God. If you haven't started your car, you can't go on a journey with God.

There are things that you need to know about salvation, which means giving your life to Jesus Christ, living for Him while you are still on Earth, and receiving the reward of eternal life in Heaven. Do you know how much God loves you? God loves you and the world so much that He gave his son, Jesus Christ, so that everyone who believes in Him will not die but will live forever in Heaven (John 3:16). You might be wondering why do we have to believe in Him in the first place or what may happen if you do not believe in Him. You read earlier that all of us have done or said bad things to others and is called sin (Romans 3:23). The proper title for people who have sinned is *sinners*. Even though we are sinners, God still loves us and wants us to be a Christ-like example while we are here on earth.

In case you are wondering what will happen if someone

chooses not to believe in Him and continues to sin, he or she will not be able to go to Heaven after life ends on Earth (Romans 6:23). If someone does not go to Heaven, they will go to place called Hell where people exist while being away from God and His goodness. If you want to live forever in Heaven, you will have to give your life to Jesus Christ. You must understand giving your life to Jesus Christ is the only way to receive the reward of eternal life in Heaven. In the Book of John (Chapter 3, verses 3-15), there was a Pharisee in the Bible named Nicodemus who was confused about being born again. Nicodemus visited Jesus late one night and acknowledged that he knew Jesus was a teacher who has come from God because of his miraculous acts. Jesus told Nicodemus that a man must be born again in order to see the Kingdom of God.

Nicodemus was probably scratching his head while asking Jesus this question, "How can a man be born again if he is old? A man cannot enter into his mother's womb a second time to be born."

Then, Jesus replied, "A person can be born again by believing that Jesus Christ is the Son of God and begin a new life with Him."

Like Nicodemus, you're probably thinking,"How can I be born again? I am already here on Earth and there is no way I can go back inside my mother." Being born again doesn't mean you will be physically born again. It means your spirit is made new and you were given a fresh start. We are going to use our imagination to understand being born again.

Imagine you bought an old car and it needed some repairs. You may need to replace the engine, tires, or other parts to make it comfortable to drive or ride in while going to your destination. You also may decide to change the paint color by adding some stripes because it is going to be your new car. It will be a similar experience with us when we give our life to God because we will have a new life and a new attitude about life which will make a Christ-like fashion statement to the world.

Becoming saved is so easy to do. It does not cost a thing or require you to do anything fancy in order to receive this gift. All you have to do is say the prayer of faith below, believe the prayer in your heart, and give your life to Him for salvation. Are YOU ready to give your life to Jesus Christ?

Say this Prayer of Faith:

"Dear God, I know I am a sinner. I believe You sent Jesus to be my Savior and that He died on the cross to take the punishment for my sins. I believe Jesus rose from the dead and is coming back someday. Please forgive me of all of my sins and come into my life and change me. Please guide me in my life and help me to follow You for the rest of my life. Thank You for saving me and taking me to heaven when I die. In Jesus's Name, Amen."

Congratulations! You are now saved. Jesus Christ is your Lord and Savior. Be sure to tell your parents or guardians and friends your good news. You are now a new Christian and will have to do certain things in order to continue to walk right in your new life. Another word you will hear people say instead of salvation or saved is that you have been **born again**. Once you give your life to Christ, new life begins. New life means that you have to become more Christ-like, stop doing things that are sinful (bad) in nature, and be a positive example for others. So you see, salvation, saved, or being born again is the key to starting your journey to **F.L.I.P.P.** your life!

CHAPTER 4: GAS (FAITH)

"We live by faith, not by sight." 2 Corinthians 5:7 NIV

The gas in the car represents our faith in God. Once we put our gas in the car, we cannot physically see the gas but we know it's there. However, cars come equipped with a gas gauge to give us an estimation of how much gas we have. If we check our gas gauge and it's near empty, we need to refuel our car by going to a gas station or we can't make it to our destination. In the same way, we have to refuel our faith through church and reading our Bible so we can do our very best in school, at home, and with friends. Colossians 3:23 says, "Whatever you do, work at it with all your heart, as working for the Lord ..." Faith works in the same way because it is believing that something is there when you cannot see it. Faith is also doing something without knowing how it is going to end, but believing that it will have a good ending.

David, a young boy who grew up to become king, was in charge of taking care of the sheep while his older brothers were away in the Isralite army. Every day, a Philistine giant, named Goliath, challenged the Israelites to fight him. The Israelite men, including David's brothers, were afraid. David accepted Goliath's challenge. He used five stones and a slingshot to fight Goliath. David believed God was going to protect him during the fight with Goliah. David defeated Goliath and became a hero.

His faith in God helped him win the challenge (1 Samuel 17).

Although we don't have a gauge to tell us how much faith we have in God, you might feel *empty* if you had a bad day at school, are having a hard time making friends, or you are having problems at home. In these bad times, you need to refuel by talking to God, going to church and reading the bible to help you overcome these problems As a Christian, faith is the gas we use to believe God is there and overcome challenges in our lives.

Chapter 5: Lights (Following Jesus)

When Jesus spoke again to the people, he said, "I am the light of the world. Whoever follows me will never walk in darkness, but will have the light of life." John 8:12 NIV

The lights on our car help us see at night and when it is foggy or rainy outside. There are lights on the inside and outside of the car. For this section, we are going to look at the headlights on the outside of the car because they are responsible for guiding us on our journey.

The headlights have two important jobs: showing us the way to go when it is hard to see and helping us avoid things that can harm ourselves, other people, and property. Jesus Christ serves as our light. He helps you to see so you will not get into trouble and guides you through the dark times of your life. At school, you may meet other kids who like to do bad things for fun but may hurt people's feelings or destroy something that is valuable to someone else. As Christians, we have to make sure we are not following people who enjoy doing bad things.

In the Bible, Jesus Christ came to a town and saw Matthew, a tax collector, working. Jesus told Matthew to follow Him and Matthew did. Matthew became a disciple of Jesus. He wrote about Jesus healing people and miracles. He also witnessed people who did not like Jesus and called him mean names.

Matthew continued to follow Jesus Christ during the good and bad times (Matthew 9, Matthew 11).

It is very important to follow Jesus Christ at all times whether we are at home, school, church, or other places we may go (John 8:12). We have to follow Jesus Christ because He is our Light that keeps us safe by helping us make good decisions and staying out of trouble. He also guides us when facing tough situations such as bad homework grades, being bullied, or if parents separate.

CHAPTER 6: ENGINE (HOLY SPIRIT)

"Since we live by the Spirit, let us keep in step with the Spirit." Galatians 5:25 NIV

Without an engine, your car is not able to run. Engines are responsible for turning gas into energy which makes the car run. People who purchase older model cars may have to replace the engine because it was broken or did not receive proper care. Car owners should be able to listen to the engine to decide if everything is okay or if it is having trouble.

The Holy Spirit in us is similar to an engine because it changes our faith in God into action. It works inside of us to keep us running and making Godly decisions (Galatians 5:25). Have you ever been so angry at someone that you wanted to yell, "Shut up!" but *something* inside of you says, "Don't say that! You're too mad. You'll either get in trouble or hurt someone, so zip your lips." The *something* inside of you telling you to make good choices is the Holy Spirit. For example, if one of your friends is bullying someone and wants to you join them, you can make a good choice by not doing it, too.

The Holy Spirit lives inside our hearts. He is the part of God that tells us to do the right thing, helps us spread the good news about Jesus Christ, and be a positive example to others in the world. Cars need gas to make the engine run. As Christians, we need to have faith in God to put the Holy Spirit in our hearts to work. The Holy Spirit is responsible for guiding our actions, behavior, thoughts, and the words we use when talking with others. As a new Christian, we will have to make changes to our *engine* by changing or replacing any bad actions, behavior, or thoughts with Christ-like ones.

Chapter 7: Steering Wheel (Prayer)

"Don't worry about anything; instead, pray about everything. Tell God what you need, and thank him for all he has done." Philipians 4:6 NIV

The steering wheel in our car is what we use to make safe turns or keep our car moving straight. It also helps us keep our car in the proper lane so we don't get into an accident. The steering wheel in our car is responsible for controlling the direction of the car. When the driver turns the steering wheel to the left or right, it sends a message to the front wheels on which way to move.

Prayer is a powerful part of our Christian walk. It is a special form of communication because it is the way we share our prayer requests with God (Philipians 4:6). The best thing about prayer is that you can pray about whatever is on your heart to God in a way that is comfortable for you. For example, you can pray out loud or silently, on your knees or sitting in a chair, alone or with a friend. Prayer is also when God comunicates with us. It's not that God talks to us like we talk to each other. When we are sitting quietly in prayer, our hearts can understand what God is telling us. Through prayer, God tells us which direction to go to stay on the right track.

Daniel, a faithful servant of God, shows a good example of prayer. Darius became king and issued a law that no one can pray to any god or person except him. Daniel continued to pray to God for the people and gave thanks to God three times a day (Daniel 6:10). Prayer can be done during good and bad times because God always listens to His people.

Sometimes, God may answer our prayers fast. Sometimes, it's at a later time. It is important to remember that God does hear our prayers and will answer them when the time is right. There may be times when God says 'no' and saying 'no' is actually an answer. Many people believe if God doesn't do what they ask of Him, He hasn't answered their prayers. But He did. He simply said no. Prayer is important for communicating with God because He steers us in the right direction.

CHAPTER 8: SEAT BELT (LOVE)

**"Above all else, guard your heart, for everything
you do flows from it." Proverbs 4:23 NIV**

The seat belt in the car protects us from getting hurt and keeps us in place if someone hits the car. The seat belt, called love, protects our heart from anger, hurt, and mean thoughts when we come against bad things or bad people.

Jesus is the best example of not only telling you what to do but showing how to do it. While Jesus Christ was on Earth, he blessed many people and performed many miracles. Most people witnessed or experienced Jesus's blessings and miracles. However, there were some people who did not believe Jesus was the Son of God. They would call Jesus bad names and accused Him of having evil spirits. Jesus Christ was able to guard his heart through all of the name calling and bullying. I bet you are wondering how Jesus was able to guard his heart. Well here's how: Jesus Christ loved all the people (and you too!) so much that He did not say a mean word back to them or did not hate them because He wanted everyone to be blessed. When some people were doing wrong, Jesus would tell them. He did that because He loved them and wanted them to stop doing bad things.

But it's different for people.

If you see another kid doing something wrong, it is best to tell an adult you trust. You may be protecting him or her from danger or hurting others. When you buckle the seat belt on your journey, you are able to guard your heart and not make bad choices when people are mean to you.

CHAPTER 9: DASHBOARD (READ YOUR BIBLE!)

"All Scripture is inspired by God and is useful to teach us what is true and to make us realize what is wrong in our lives. It corrects us when we are wrong and teaches us to do what is right." 2 Timothy 3:16-17 NIV

The dashboard in the car gives the driver a lot of information about the car such as how fast the car is going, how much gas you have left, and when the car needs maintenance. Your Bible is your dashboard. Once you give your life to Jesus Christ, you are trading in your old car (old life) for your new car (new life). People are not able to learn everything about their new car without reading the owner's manual. They may be able to drive the car but will not be able to enjoy the features of the car or learn the warning signs to look for when the car is having problems.

The Bible is the most important book you will need for the rest of your new life. It is our owner's manual and contains the Word of God to help us become more Christ-like and guide us on our journey. The Bible has 66 different books that were combined into one special book. God chose these special people to write His Word, called Scriptures, to give us valuable information that will prepare us to be positive examples for others in everything we do as a child and an adult. It is a good idea to read the Bible like reading the owner's manual. The Bible helps us to get to know God better. It is important to understand God's love for us and to get to know Him better. The Bible contains important information about how people in the Bible were blessed, the life of Jesus, what to do when you are having problems, and other useful information. You need to read now and forever to learn more about God and how He is there for us during the good and bad times.

CHAPTER 10: BRAKES (FORGIVENESS)

"For if you forgive other people when they sin against you, your heavenly Father will also forgive you."
Matthew 6:14 NIV

The brakes on the car are used to either slow down or stop a vehicle from running into another car or things. Also, it keeps the people in the car safe from being harmed. Forgiveness is the brakes we use to keep us from hurting other people. Sometimes, we may face situations that will hurt our feelings such as getting into an argument with our best friend or a little brother or sister destroying a favorite movie or video game. Even though we get hurt or angry, we have to stop and forgive before our anger makes things worse. Think about this…we are not perfect and may do something to others that will hurt or make them angry.

As a Christian, I would like to know that I can apologize for doing something wrong to others and have them forgive me. Forgiveness, whether it is asking to be forgiven or accepting someone's apology is not an easy thing to do. It can take some time to get over or forget the bad situation. In the Bible, Jesus tells the story of a man who had two sons. The younger son asked for his part of the inheritance. The older son remained home and continued taking care of his house and his father. The younger son then left home and used all the money on doing fun things. He had to return home because he had no food. He felt bad for making bad choices and asked his father for forgiveness. The father forgave him and welcomed him home with a big party (Luke 15:11-24).

The older son, however, was very upset because his dad never threw him a party even though he stayed and continued taking care of the home. The older son had a hard time forgiving his dad because he felt as though his dad did not care that he did the right thing. He also had a hard time forgiving his brother for running off and wasting all his money. If you are having a hard time forgiving someone, pray to God and ask Him to help you forgive the person and free your mind from bad feelings.

We have to forgive as God forgave us for all of the bad things that we did to others and against Him. Forgiveness is not for the other person. It's for ourselves. Sometimes, people will not ask for forgiveness, but when we forgive them anyway, we become more like Jesus. And forgiving someone doesn't mean you have to be their best friend. It sometimes means you aren't friends, but you don't think mean things about them anymore.

Acts 2:42

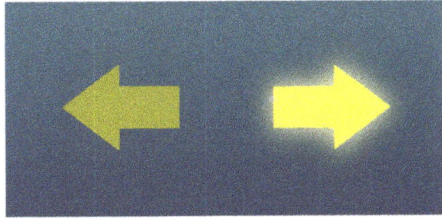
Deuteronomy 10:22

Acts 20:35

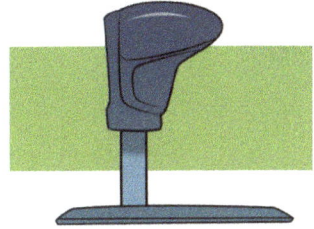
Proverbs 3:5–6

Psalm 34:1

Matthew 14:23

96.5

Mark 14:23

Colossians 2:12–14

CHAPTER 11: WHEELS (ATTEND CHURCH)

"They devoted themselves to the apostles' teaching and to fellowship, to the breaking of bread and to prayer."
Acts 2:42 NIV

The wheels of the car help the car frame and its parts move in the right direction. The wheels of the car are designed to work together with the steering wheel to help passengers get to their destination. Just as wheels keep your car moving, attending church helps us move in the right direction with Jesus. When we attend church, we have a *family* to help encourage us to keep moving in the right direction.

Church attendance allows us to set aside special time with other members to grow our faith and make us spiritually strong during bad times. The members in the church are called family because they all share the same beliefs and gather together to hear the Word of God, sing worship songs, pray together, and fellowship. Church is similar to school because it has a preacher who gives lessons, called sermons, to the members to either encourage them to make good choices or remind them what happens when they make bad choices. The preacher also helps us understand God's Word and build our spiritual strength to help during challenges.

By attending church, the members are able to come together

and show their love and worship to God. The preacher and members can honor, praise, and thank God in public with other people that share the same believe and love for God. Going to church encourages others on their journey with God, welcome new members to the church family, and provide support to members who are going through good or bad times.

CHAPTER 12: TURN SIGNALS (OBEY)

"You must love the LORD your God and obey all his requirements, laws, regulations, and commands."
Deuteronomy 10:22 NIV

Turn signals on cars are used to let people behind or in front of you know that you are getting ready to turn either left or right. Drivers have to select the signal early before making the turn to give the other drivers enough notice about which way the car is going to turn. Whichever signal you choose to use, you are expected to turn that way because if you turn the other way, you can cause an accident.

An interesting fact about obeying people in charge, laws, or rules, is that we receive instructions on what or what not to do before we actually have to do it. You need to make sure that you are using your turn signals and listening to God, your parents, teachers, etc., because if you do not, you can cause something bad to happen to you or others.

Noah, a man in the Bible, loved and obeyed God laws. One day, God spoke to Noah about building an ark to hold his family and animals because a great flood was coming to the land. God told Noah how big to build the ark, what type of wood to use, and which animals to place on the ark. Noah obeyed God, finished the ark, and loaded the animals on the ark. A few days later, it rained and flooded the land. Noah, his family, and the animals were safe (Genesis 7:6-10). People who love God and are willing to obey the laws on Earth and in the Bible can be good examples to others by encouraging them to obey the laws too!

CHAPTER 13: CAR SEATS
(SERVING AND GIVING)

"…You should remember the words of the Lord Jesus: 'It is more blessed to give than to receive." Acts 20:35 NIV

The seats in the car carry us while on our journey. They are designed to support the body in the sitting position. Sometimes the journey may be a short trip, such as going to the grocery store. Sometimes it's a longer road trip like a family vacation. In both cases, the driver and passengers should be comfortable to truly enjoy the journey. Our seats of serving and giving are the gifts inside of us, such as helping others, that will allow us to be a comfort to others.

Once we are saved, the seats we have are used to make others comfortable. Think of it this way: We received the key of salvation and now are the drivers of our new car. We want our passengers (other people who are saved or not saved) to experience the comfort of Christ-like serving and giving. Moses, one of God's servants, was responsible for leading the Israelities to freedom from slavery under King Pharaoh. Along the journey, the Israelites traveled though Amalek and encountered very bad people called the Amalekites. The Amalekites were mad that Moses and the Israelites were traveling through their land and challenged them to war. The Israelites were so afraid of the Amalekites that they forgot the power of God! In order to help the Israelites remember God was still with them, Moses went on top of the hill and held his rod toward God. Moses's arms began to get weak from holding the rod, so Aaron and Hur used their arms to hold Moses's arms up until they won the fight (Exodus 17:8-12). By serving or giving to others, we are able to show the love of God.

The Bible says it is more blessed to give than to receive. You might think you will be more comfortable if you receive, but you will actually feel better to give. Do you want others to enjoy riding in your car seats? Serving and giving are some things you can do anytime or anywhere. You can do it at home by doing chores or extra household duties without being told. Also, you can give by serving in the community doing things like participating in a park clean-up project, working in a soup kitchen, or by singing in the choir at church.

CHAPTER 14: GEAR SHIFT (TRUST)

"Trust in the LORD with all your heart and lean not on your own understanding; in all your ways acknowledge him, and he will make your paths straight." Proverbs 3:5-6 NIV

The gear shift makes the engine run smoother at different speeds. It also helps cars adjust to the right speed to drive up and down steep hills and through any road conditions. Sometimes in life, God wants us to show our trust in Him by *slowing down* to pray and talk with Him and *speeding up* to listen to his Word. Sometimes in life we have to remain *neutral* and not participate in bad things, and *reverse* and reflect on our actions and how they affected others. The more we trust God with our lives, or the better our gear shifts, the better equipped we are to make it through rough road conditions, or tough situations in our lives.

The story of Joseph shows us a great example of trusting God at all times (Genesis 30-50). Joseph's brothers were jealous of him because he was their father's favorite child. The brothers played a mean trick on Joseph and then threw him in a pit. Joseph trusted God for delievery out of the pit. The brothers sold him into slavery and took him away from the family. He was sold to Potiphar, an official to Pharaoh's house. Joseph was a blessing to the household until Potiphar's wife lied about him which landed him in prison. Joseph had the gift of interpreting, or explaining dreams, so Pharoah released him from prison and placed him in charge of the people. Joseph was reunited with his family and blessed them because of his trust in God through all his the challenges.

Just like the people in the Bible, we can trust God with different things in our lives, even if things look bad. We can pray and believe in Him to shift our gear in the right direction, get over challenges, and soar over bumps in the road during our journey on Earth. It is important that we trust God in all directions of our life.

CHAPTER 15: CAR DOORS
(PRAISE AND WORSHIP)

**"I will extol (bless/praise) the Lord at all times;
his praise will always be on my lips." Psalm 34:1 NIV**

The doors on our car allow us to get into the car, keep us in the car while we are on our journey, and open when we reach our destination. Car doors can be opened manually by passengers or automatically using a button or knob that is designed to secure or release the door lock. In our car, the doors represent praise and worship.

We can praise and worship God by listening to Christian music, singing a Christian song, and can even praise and worship Him quietly such as spending time in prayer. The doors of our car open to let the love and knowledge of God into us, secure it inside of us so nobody can take it from us (unless we let them… which is a no-no), and close to allow us to use it whenever we want to use it. Another great feature about our doors is that we're able to open them to receive what God says to us through praise and worship songs. And we can close them to anything that does not honor God. Sometimes our doors will be opened and closed automatically by God to receive more praise and worship through His word, songs, and books.

Our Scripture for this chapter, Psalm 34:1, tells us that we should praise the Lord at all times (you should underline or highlight the words *all times* in the scripture). Since we share this earth with around seven billion people, there are times when we will be happy, sad, angry, and encounter situations that that can either make or spoil our day. No matter how you feel, you can praise and worship God because He is the only one who can truly help you. God loves you so much that you can go to Him anytime, spend time with Him in prayer, attend Bible study or worship Him through reading, thinking, or singing to help change bad feelings into good ones.

CHAPTER 16: OIL (DEVOTION)

"After he (Jesus) had dismissed them, he went up on a mountainside by himself to pray. Later that night, he was there alone ..." Matthew 14:23 NIV

Oil keeps our car running smoothly. It is responsible for lubricating (applying grease) to different parts of the engine. Oil keeps the engine clean, cool, and protects its parts in order to get the best performance and extend the life of the engine. If a car does not have its oil changed or runs out of oil, the car will ride very bumpy and eventually breakdown. It is important that we have devotion time with God.

Devotion time allows us to build our relationship with God. When you were saved, you started a new life with Jesus Christ. A friendship with Jesus Christ has been formed. Once we make a new friend, we want to learn more about them like their favorite hobby, television show, or food. Sometimes you and your new friend will spend time alone doing fun things, talking about different things, and sharing stories or secrets with each other. The Scripture at the beginning of the chapter tells us that even Jesus Christ spent time alone with God. He took time away from His disciples, or His friends, to pray and spend quiet time with God. A relationship with Jesus works the same. There are several things you can do to improve your relationship with God such as reading the Bible, memorizing Scriptures, and writing about how

God has blessed you in a journal.

Just like the oil for our car, we have to spend time with God to clean our hearts and mind, cool our attitude if we are sad or upset, and learn how to protect ourselves from harm. Without taking time out to learn about Him, our life will be very bumpy and eventually break down.

CHAPTER 17: RADIO (EVANGELISM/TELLING OTHERS ABOUT GOD)

"He (Jesus) said to them, "Go into all the world and preach the gospel to all creation." Mark 14:23 NIV

The radio in your car serves as a communication device that sends information using sound waves from one place to another. It allows you to hear music, listen to the news and weather information. Jesus Christ told his disciples to go tell people about his Gospel, or good news. Since we are Jesus's disciples, we should spread the good news about Him to everyone in our reach.

Can you imagine if disciples from all over the world would share the Gospel? More people would be given an opportunity to get a new life and receive the key to their car. Then, they will be able to reach other people! Everybody will hear about the benefits of giving their lives to God which is an eternal place in Heaven. You will be the *radio* for God and tell others about our Lord and Savior Jesus Christ.

Paul, one of the greatest leaders and authors in the Bible, went to Philippi to speak to the people. He went outside the city's gates to speak to the women about God. Lydia heard Paul's message about God and wanted to become a believer in Jesus (Acts 16:11-15).

There are so many ways to share the Gospel with others. Some ways are to talk about Jesus Christ while playing with friends, tell parents and other family members who are not saved about how Jesus Christ helped you during bad times. You can even go door-to-door with an outreach group from church. You can be creative and find other ways to share the Gospel with others. As Christians, we are to go into the world, tell others about Jesus Christ, and give the key (tell them about salvation) so they can **F.L.I.P.P.** their lives, too!

CHAPTER 18: CAR WASH (BAPTISM)

"For you were buried with Christ when you were baptized. And with him you were raised to new life because you trusted the mighty power of God, who raised Christ from the dead. You were dead because of your sins and because your sinful nature was not yet cut away. Then God made you alive with Christ, for he forgave all our sins." Colossians 2:12-14 NIV

Car washes are used to clean the outside of cars by removing dirt, mud, and other stains from the car to make it shiny again. Once a new car is purchased, the dealer washes the car before the person takes it home. The dealer will also clean the car on the inside to make it new for the owner. A car wash for us is baptism.

Some people are baptized at church or in a lake, and some people are baptized by pouring or sprinking, too. Baptism represents washing away our sins and the beginning of a life with Jesus. When we are raised out of the water, it makes us clean on the inside and we begin our new life with Christ. After we give our life to Christ, we are baptized as an outward sign of our faith. Baptism cleans our soul on the inside by taking away our past sins and allowing us start our new life with a clean slate. When Paul became a follower of God, Ananias told him to get baptized to wash his past sins away and tell others about God (Acts 22:14-16). Our baptism shows the world that we are true disciples of God.

Our Lord and Savior Jesus Christ was baptized. He was baptized not because of His sins because He was without sin. Jesus Christ was baptized to set an example of showing obedience to God's plan for our new life and way of thinking.

Chapter 19: The End of this Book and the Beginning of Your New Life

Congratulations! You finally reached the end of this book and now you are ready to begin your new life with God. Before you gave your life to Christ, you were an old, beat up car that was either not running or running right. After you gave your life to Christ, you became a shiny, new car and ready to take the ride of your life. You have *flipped*, or changed, the way you act, think, and do things for yourself and others. In order to stay shiny and new, you will have to take time out to review the things in this book.

<u>Let's review all the parts of our new car</u>

- The key to the car represents salvation, or accepting Jesus into your life, which is where the exciting journey begins!

- Gas is the faith needed to help us to on on journey with Jesus Christ through good and bad times.

- The headlights help people make good, safe decisions when it is dark outside. Following Jesus helps us make good, safe decisions that keep us out of darkness.

- The engine of the car is the Holy Spirit, which turns our faith into action by guiding us to make positive decisions.

- The steering wheel represents prayer, which is when we

talk to God and ask Him for direction.

- Just as a seat belt goes across the heart and protects the driver and passengers, our spiritual seat belt of love shields our hearts and protects us from bad choices when people are mean to us.

- The dashboard of a car contains a lot of very important information about our car. Our Bible, like the dashboard of a car, teaches us how to operate with a Christ-like mind.

- The brakes on a car represent forgiveness. When someone says or does something mean to us, we shouldn't say or do anything mean back. Instead, we should stop and forgive those who hurt us because it is what Jesus would do.

- The wheels on a car represent going to church because going to church not only gives us time to be with other believers, it also helps us to continue moving in the right direction.

- The turn signals remind us to be obedient and follow directions.

- The seats of serving and giving are the gifts inside of us, such as helping others, that will allow us to be a comfort to others.

- The gear shift on a vehicle allows us to adjust our speed to varying road conditions. As a Christian, the gear shift is our trust in God.

- The doors of our car represent praise and worship, because through praise and worship, we have the power to open up our car doors to let the love and knowledge of God into us or close them off to anything that does not honor God.

- The oil keeps the engine running smoothly by keeping it cool, clean, and free from rust, which can cause the car to break down. Devotion time with God prevents our spirit from breaking down.

- The radio is a communication device that is used to deliver music, news, and messages to the people. Chrisitians use evangelism to spread the Good News of Jesus Christ to the people.

- Baptism represents washing away our sins on the outside and inside.

Prayer of Commitment

"God, I am going to **F.L.I.P.P.** my life today, and have Faithful Learning In Public and Private for you today and always."

Please tell others how to **F.L.I.P.P.** their lives too!

DISCUSSION QUESTIONS
FOR F.L.I.P.P. YOUR LIFE

1. What did you enjoy about the book?

2. The acronym **F.L.I.P.P.** represents what group of words?

3. Why do you think the author chose this title for the book?

4. What does the old car represent?

5. What does the new car represent?

6. Name the car parts and their meaning.

7. What does salvation mean? Are you saved?

8. Give some examples to be Christ-like in public.

9. Give some examples of being Christ-like in private.

10. Describe how you show the love of God to others.

11. Name three Biblical characters used as examples in this book.

12. Describe a time when you faced a challenge. How did you overcome it?

13. Why is having faith important?

14. How do you plan to **F.L.I.P.P.** your life?

15. If you had to describe this book to a family member or friend, what would you say?